HAZARDOUS TRASH

By Melissa Raé Shofner

Gareth Stevens
PUBLISHING

Please visit our website, www.garethstevens.com. For a free color catalog of all our high-quality books, call toll free 1-800-542-2595 or fax 1-877-542-2596.

Library of Congress Cataloging-in-Publication Data

Names: Shofner, Melissa Raé, author.
Title: Hazardous trash / Melissa Raé Shofner.
Description: New York : Gareth Stevens Publishing, [2018] | Series: Unnatural disasters | Includes bibliographical references and index.
Identifiers: LCCN 2016059150| ISBN 9781538204368 (pbk. book) | ISBN 9781538204375 (6 pack) | ISBN 9781538204382 (library bound book)
Subjects: LCSH: Hazardous waste sites–Juvenile literature.
Classification: LCC TD1030.5 .S56 2018 | DDC 363.72/88–dc23
LC record available at https://lccn.loc.gov/2016059150

First Edition

Published in 2018 by
Gareth Stevens Publishing
111 East 14th Street, Suite 349
New York, NY 10003

Copyright © 2018 Gareth Stevens Publishing

Designer: Sam DeMartin
Editor: Joan Stoltman

Photo credits: Cover, p. 1 Corbis Historical/Getty Images; p. 5 Comstock/Getty Images; p. 7 (top) Stuart Dee/Getty Images; p. 7 (bottom) Dipak Shelare/Shutterstock.com; p. 8 EBPhoto/Shutterstock.com; p. 9 SIMON MAINA/AFP/Getty Images; p. 11 (top) Alejo Miranda/Shutterstock.com; p. 11 (bottom) Andrei Tudoran/Shutterstock.com; p. 13 Laurence Fordyce/Getty Images; pp. 14, 15 GeorginaCaptures/Shutterstock.com; p. 16 ORLANDO SIERRA/AFP/Getty Images; p. 17 © iStockphoto.com/Robert_Ford; p. 19 Feifei Cui-Paoluzza/Getty Images; p. 21 Peter Essick/Getty Images; p. 23 (top) D_Townsend/Shutterstock.com; p. 23 (bottom) TFoxFoto/Shutterstock.com; pp. 24, 25 Rich Carey/Shutterstock.com; p. 27 (Earth) visdia/Shutterstock.com; p. 27 (debris) Deviney Designs/Shutterstock.com; p. 29 Trikona/Shutterstock.com.

Printed in China

CPSIA compliance information: Batch #CS17GS: For further information contact Gareth Stevens, New York, New York at 1-800-542-2595.

CONTENTS

Words in the glossary appear in **bold** type
the first time they are used in the text.

A GROWING PROBLEM

At some point, you've probably been asked to take out the **garbage**. Do you know where that trash goes after it's trucked away each week? More than 250 million tons (227 million mt) of household trash are created in the United States each year. That's enough trash to fill 63,000 garbage trucks every day. More than half of this waste, called **municipal** solid waste (MSW), ends up in a dump. MSW has become a huge problem around the world.

As populations grow and countries develop, there are more people using more goods and creating more waste. The harmful effects are being felt by people, plants, and animals everywhere. Is it too late to save our planet from being buried in garbage?

UNITED STATES WASTE BY THE NUMBERS

- 5 percent of the world's population creates 30 percent of the world's MSW, which is 254 million tons (230 million mt) yearly
- each American averages 4.4 pounds (2 kg) of MSW daily
- each American averages 90,000 pounds (41,000 kg) of MSW in their lifetime
- states with the most trash per person: Nevada, Pennsylvania, Colorado, California
- 28 billion pounds (13 billion kg) of food waste yearly
- 360 billion pounds (163 billion kg) of chemical waste from manufacturing yearly

LASTING EFFECT

MSW is from home, work, school, and restaurants. **Hazardous** waste includes paint, cleaning supplies, and batteries. Electronic waste, or e-waste, includes old electronics. Medical waste includes used needles and bandages from hospitals or doctors' offices.

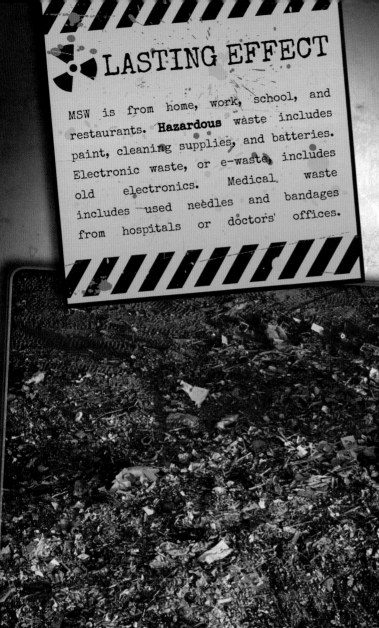

The Fresh Kills Landfill in Staten Island, New York, used to be the largest garbage dump on Earth, with up to 29,000 tons (26,308 mt) of trash dumped daily. Now it's being made into a park!

WASTE PICKERS

Many of the largest, most toxic garbage dumps are located in developing countries. Landfills, or dumps, are usually near major cities, and areas surrounding the dumps are often slums. Slums are dirty, rundown parts of a city that are very poor.

Around the world, millions of people from slums sort trash to earn a living. These people, called waste pickers, look for items that can be sold, recycled, reused, and even eaten. The adults and children who work as waste pickers are exposed to many dangerous things. The surrounding land, air, and water are heavily polluted by MSW, and waste pickers often don't wear masks or gloves while sorting through the trash. Many develop health issues such as breathing problems.

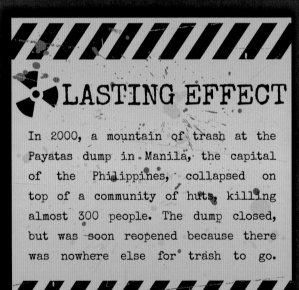

LASTING EFFECT

In 2000, a mountain of trash at the Payatas dump in Manila, the capital of the Philippines, collapsed on top of a community of huts, killing almost 300 people. The dump closed, but was soon reopened because there was nowhere else for trash to go.

The waste pickers of Payatas belong to one of several city labor groups, which gives them fairer hours and training and bans children from working.

MAKING A DIFFERENCE

Waste pickers deal with unsafe conditions every day for very little pay. They are informally employed, which means their jobs aren't overseen by the government and their work is risky. However, by sorting through trash to find recyclable items, they're helping the **environment**, contributing to public health and safety, and supporting local economies. Some places are recognizing the important work of waste pickers and are pushing to include them in organized waste-management programs.

7

THE DANDORA DUMPSITE

Dandora is the main dump of Nairobi, Kenya, a city with almost 4 million residents. Its waste pickers earn between 60¢ and $6.00 a day. It's a major event at Dandora when garbage trucks come with food scraps. These food scraps become meals for those brave enough—and strong enough—to fight their way through the hungry crowds that form around the trucks.

DANDORA KEY INFORMATION

- **what:** a 30-acre (12 ha) dump containing MSW, hazardous waste, and medical waste

- **where:** Nairobi, Kenya, including residential areas and the surrounding environment

- **when:** 1975 to present

- **how much:** over 2,200 tons (2,000 mt) dumped daily

- **people affected:** around 2 million people live in the slums and 56 percent of Nairobi's population, or 2.2 million people, live along the polluted Nairobi River

According to international environmental laws, Dandora should have closed in 1990. But no one enforced these laws, so it remains open even today. It was even declared full in 2001, but dumping continued. In 2016, workers trying to create more space at the dump stopped working and instead protested because they weren't being paid. This, however, didn't stop the trash from coming.

LASTING EFFECT

Dandora poisons the Nairobi River, a body of water 242 miles (390 km) long that, among other things, is used for drinking water. It flows into the Indian Ocean, and we have no idea what effects the pollution causes.

This image shows people searching for things to sell and animals looking for food in the trash at Dandora.

DANGERS IN BOLIVIA

K'ara K'ara, a landfill in Bolivia, doesn't have a protective liner underneath, and there's no drain system in place. This means there's nothing stopping toxic liquids in the garbage from collecting in pools or seeping into the earth beneath the dumpsite.

What began as 120 people is now around 5,000 waste pickers risking **infections**, skin diseases, **cancer**, and more by working here. An area for dumping medical waste was once fenced off, but now even used needles, bloody bandages, and more are picked through in hopes of finding trash. People continue to build homes near K'ara K'ara because they don't know just how toxic the dumpsite is.

LASTING EFFECT

The site was supposed to be closed in 2003, but wasn't. In 2009, the government of the nearby city decided to close K'ara K'ara and open a new dumpsite that has the proper liner beneath it. The cost to clean up K'ara K'ara may be around $5.8 million.

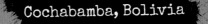

K'ARA K'ARA KEY INFORMATION

- **what:** a 62-acre (25 ha) dump containing MSW and medical waste

- **where:** Cochabamba, Bolivia

- **when:** 1987 to present

- **how much:** 500 tons (454 mt) dumped daily; 3.1 to 4.4 million tons (2.8 to 4 million mt) of waste total

- **people affected:** around 670,000 residents of Cochabamba

- **other problems:** toxic methane gas, released by MSW when it breaks down, sometimes catches fire, setting the garbage on fire and creating toxic smoke

A POORLY PLANNED CITY

Santo Domingo is the largest city and the capital of the Dominican Republic. It's home to 2.9 million people and produces half of the entire country's MSW. Unfortunately, the poorly planned layout of the city makes it hard for garbage trucks to do their job.

Duquesa, the Dominican Republic's largest landfill, is in Santo Domingo. Garbage trucks have trouble dumping trash there because roads inside the dump are badly in need repair. Because the city's roads are also in bad shape, garbage trucks often can't get down all the streets. So residents have created smaller dumps throughout the city and thrown trash into the streets and waterways. **Sewers** clogged with waste cause flooding in many areas, and health problems from dirty water are common.

DUQUESA KEY INFORMATION

- **what:** a 316-acre (128 ha) dump containing MSW and hazardous waste

- **where:** Santo Domingo, Dominican Republic

- **when:** unknown to present

- **how much:** nearly 4,000 tons (3,629 mt) dumped daily

- **why:** sanitary landfills, where waste is processed and safe, are too expensive for poor countries like the Dominican Republic to build

LASTING EFFECT

Several companies from around the world have offered to help turn Duquesa into a sanitary landfill. One company was hired, but after 4 years of improvements to Duquesa, only 1 percent of the recyclable trash is actually getting recycled.

The small dumpsites that people make throughout the Dominican Republic pollute the environment and poison the people and animals.

UPSETTING THE LOCALS

Bantar Gebang is a landfill 25 miles (40 km) outside of Jakarta, the capital of Indonesia. Jakarta's 10.3 million residents make enough trash to dump there day and night nowadays. But it wasn't always this way: Jakarta gained 7 million residents between 2000 and 2010 and is now a "megacity."

This river filled with MSW runs through a slum in Jakarta.

LASTING EFFECT

Sadly, over 2,000 families work at Bantar Gebang, including mothers, fathers, and children—some as young as 5! About 1,500 shacks have been built on Bantar Gebang by pickers. Some even find their food in the waste.

BANTAR GEBANG KEY INFORMATION

- **what:** a 276.8-acre (112 ha) dump containing MSW

- **where:** Bekasi, outside of Jakarta, Indonesia

- **when:** 1989 to present

- **how much:** 7,165 tons (6,500 mt) dumped daily

- **other problems:** no laws exist in Indonesia to stop children from working in dumps; their after-school job gives them lung problems, skin issues, injuries, and intestinal worms

What started as 120 waste pickers in 1988 has grown to 6,000 today. Without a recycling program in the city, the residents of Jakarta don't understand how recycling works, and have no place to do it anyway. Plus, Bantar Gebang is far enough outside the city that people in Jakarta don't see how full it is and how much trash continues to be dumped every day. If they visited the dump, the smell alone would be enough to make them demand change!

WASTE PICKERS GET HELP

Trash Mountain Project (TMP) is a group created in 2009. Their goal is to help the waste pickers and improve the slums waste pickers live in. TMP provides healthy food, medical care, and education to waste pickers and their families in five countries, including Honduras.

More than 1,500 waste pickers both live and work in the Tegucigalpa landfill of Honduras, often in temperatures over 100°F (37.8°C)! Men, women, and children work in the dump as waste pickers, their homes built from scraps found in the dump, their meals often coming from food scraps found while working. At Tegucigalpa, TMP has set up an on-site health clinic, built 12 homes, sent 175 children to school, and provided lunch for the workers during the workweek.

Pollution is a major issue in all of Honduras, not just in Tegucigalpa.

TEGUCIGALPA KEY INFORMATION

- **what:** a 99-acre (40 ha) dump, the size of 130 football fields, containing MSW, medical waste, and hazardous waste

- **where:** Tegucigalpa, the capital of Honduras, the second-poorest country in Central America

- **when:** 1977 to present

- **who is affected:** 850,000 to 1.6 million residents of Tegucigalpa, 55 percent living in slums

- **people affected:** at least 2,200 killed; 30,000 to 40,000 ill

- **other problems:** 40 percent of Tegucigalpa residents have no **access** to city garbage collection services, so they dump garbage into the streets and rivers

LASTING EFFECT

Honduras is a very unsafe place for environmental **activists**. One report states that 101 activists were killed in Honduras between 2010 and 2014.

TRAGEDY AT THE LANDFILL

Estrutural is the largest dumpsite in Brazil, found near the capital city of Brasília. In some parts of this enormous dump, trash is piled 197 feet (60 m) high! Many of the waste pickers working at Estrutural also live there. There are organized groups of waste pickers, and child labor isn't allowed. However, children are still often found sorting through trash in the dumpsite.

LASTING EFFECT

The Brazilian government has been working to close Estrutural since 2005 and has fined the owners of the landfill $5 million. The site was supposed to close in 2014 and be replaced with a new sanitary landfill, but that didn't happen.

Working conditions for waste pickers at Estrutural are very dangerous. There have been numerous accidents and deaths. A waste picker's leg was crushed by a wagon in 2013. In 2014, four workers died after being run over by a tractor. At least one worker died in a similar accident at the dump in 2015.

ESTRUTURAL KEY INFORMATION

- **what:** a dump covering over 336 acres (136 ha) containing MSW and construction waste

- **where:** Brasília, Brazil

- **when:** mid-1960s to present

- **how much:** over 7,400 tons (6,700 mt) dumped daily; 33 million tons (30 million mt) total

- **people affected:** 2,700 waste pickers; nearly 3 million residents

- **other problems:** the rats, dogs, vultures, and cockroaches of Estrutural spread diseases to the protected animals of the National Park of Brasília, only 0.3 mile (0.5 km) away

Estrutural, Brazil

The toxic, damaged Estrutural slum is the only home many of the local waste pickers have ever known.

"E" IS FOR ENVIRONMENTAL HARM

AGBOGBLOSHIE KEY INFORMATION

- **what:** a 26.2-acre (10.6 ha) dump containing e-waste

- **where:** Accra, Ghana

- **how much:** an estimated hundreds of thousands of tons dumped yearly

- **people affected:** 40,000 waste pickers from all over western Africa; 79,000 residents in a nearby slum who are continuously exposed to toxic smoke from the dump

- **other problems:** waste pickers are injured, burned, diseased, and poisoned by the e-waste, often dying of cancer before age 30

New **technology** is developing constantly, and people love to get the newest technology as soon as it's in stores. But where do all the outdated devices go? Ghana's Agbogbloshie dump is the largest e-waste dump in the world. E-waste, which contains leaky old batteries and all sorts of metals, among other things, can be safely recycled, but this doesn't happen in Agbogbloshie.

Biggest E-Waste Generators in 2014 (lbs per capita)

Country	lbs per capita
NORWAY	62.4
SWITZERLAND	58.0
ICELAND	57.3
DENMARK	52.9
UNITED KINGDOM	51.8
NETHERLANDS	51.4
SWEDEN	49.2
FRANCE	48.9
UNITED STATES	48.7
AUSTRIA	48.6

E-waste from other countries, including the United States, is illegally dumped at Agbogbloshie, too!

In October 2014, a company called Pure Earth announced that it was starting e-waste recycling at Agbogbloshie. They strip wires off dumped technology items and then remove the valuable metal inside the wiring. Since metals are so toxic, this process greatly reduces the amount of toxins released into the environment around Agbogbloshie when e-waste is burned.

LASTING EFFECT

Several international laws, some created even before Agbogbloshie opened, have tried to make dumping e-waste in poor countries by rich countries illegal. Sadly, the e-waste recycling program in Agbogbloshie is a rare success for e-waste activists.

ULAB RECYCLING

A kind of e-waste from a certain car battery—called a used lead-acid battery (ULAB)—is very dangerous to recycle safely. The metal inside these batteries can be reused and is quite valuable. Some poorer countries see them as an opportunity and buy large quantities of ULABs for hired workers to recycle.

But when ULAB recycling isn't regulated, waste pickers sometimes do that recycling right in their home or yard! The process involves breaking open the batteries with an axe or by hand. Battery acid can easily spill onto the ground and seep into the soil. The removed lead is then melted down using a stove, creating toxic smoke and lead dust, which gets into the air, soil, and water of the surrounding area.

LEAD POISONING

Exposure to lead, called lead poisoning, causes many health issues. It's especially common in babies and toddlers because they often put their hands in their mouth. The many terrible side effects include headaches, bone and muscle problems, delays in growth, memory loss, and even brain damage. In extreme cases, lead poisoning causes death. Several activist groups are focused on cleaning up affected areas and educating people about the dangers of lead.

CAUTION LEAD HAZARD

The lead in car batteries is one of many heavy metals, which are metals that occur in nature and are toxic to people.

☢ LASTING EFFECT

Millions of people around the world are estimated to be affected by the lead pollution created by ULAB recycling.

GARBAGE IN EARTH'S OCEANS

TRASH OVERBOARD!

Ships, including those of the US Navy, are allowed to throw some types of trash into the ocean, but there are very strict laws about what kind. Laws usually allow food scraps and paper waste to be tossed overboard because they will break down without causing much harm to the ocean environment. A ship that is following the law will store their other garbage, such as plastic waste, until the ship returns to shore.

Earth's oceans have a plastic problem. In early 2015, it was estimated that the oceans contain around 5.25 **trillion** pieces of plastic trash. Scientists know about 70 percent of this plastic trash sinks, but estimate about 269,000 tons (244,000 mt) of that waste remains on the surface of the world's oceans.

Marine garbage collects in five separate areas of the Pacific, the Atlantic, and the Indian Oceans. The largest area, which stretches between North America and Japan, was discovered in 1997 and is called the Great Pacific Garbage Patch. Scientists know ocean trash is harmful to animals that may eat it or become caught in it. However, more research is needed to figure out how plastic harms ocean environments as it breaks down.

LASTING EFFECT

Plastic trash has even been found frozen in Arctic ice. It's estimated that over 8 million tons (7.3 million mt) of plastic waste are dumped into the ocean each year, even though it's illegal to do so.

Because over 70 percent of Earth's surface is covered in water, it took scientists 4 years and dozens of trips around the world in ships to find out the amount of plastic in the oceans.

BEYOND EARTH

Unfortunately, trash piling up on land and water isn't the end of this sad story. There's also trash in space! Space junk, the term for this garbage, may also mean rocks and debris from colliding stars and dying planets. But man-made space junk, including old spacecraft and debris from space missions, isn't only unnatural—it's unsafe!

The National Aeronautics and Space Administration (NASA) **monitors** more than 500,000 pieces of space junk circling Earth, 21,000 of which are over 4 inches (10 cm) large. Many pieces are small, but they orbit at up to 17,500 miles (28,163.5 km) per hour. If debris gets too close to a spacecraft, NASA typically needs many hours to move the spacecraft out of harm's way!

CLEANING UP SPACE JUNK

Any time two things collide in space, many smaller pieces of debris are created. Is there any way to clean up outer space? NASA and a few other space programs are trying to reduce debris by designing spacecraft that won't contribute so many pieces of new space junk to the mass of old space junk. Many other ideas, including one involving **lasers**, have been proposed, but they're all very expensive.

WHAT'S **SPACE JUNK** MADE OF?

17%
rocket
debris

19%
debris from
missions

22%
broken
spacecraft

42%
pieces from
broken
spacecraft

LASTING EFFECT

Space junk sometimes drops out of orbit and falls down toward Earth. Thankfully, it usually burns up in the atmosphere's gases.

HOW CAN YOU HELP?

A BIGGER IMPACT

The items we use every day affect the environment in many ways long before they end up in a landfill. The machinery and factories that make new products burn many different kinds of fuels, creating toxic smoke and causing pollution. Precious natural resources that we need to live, like water and trees, are often used in factory processes as well. Reducing, reusing, and recycling save energy and resources, helping animals, people, and the whole planet!

As Earth's population increases, so does its waste problem. MSW and other kinds of waste are piling up around the world at an alarming rate. But you can help!

You've probably heard the saying "reduce, reuse, recycle" before. One of the easiest things you can do to lessen the amount of trash you create is to reduce the amount of things you use because using fewer things equals less waste. The next best thing is to reuse items whenever possible, like clothes, backpacks, and electronics. Finally, you can recycle items that you use and help others recycle at home and school. You could even join an environmental activism club at school. If there isn't one, start your own!

RECYCLING NUMBERS IN THE
UNITED STATES

Even though half the trash in this country can be recycled, only 2 percent is!

Of the 35 billion plastic bottles Americans throw out yearly, 96 million daily, only 25 percent are recycled plastic. If they all were, 1 billion gallons (3.8 billion L) of oil would be saved yearly.

Cardboard and paper make up 41 percent of MSW in the United States. Sunday newspapers use over 500,000 trees, and 88 percent of those papers aren't recycled.

Recycled glass takes 30 percent less energy to make, enough to run a lightbulb for 4 hours per bottle!

Cans from recycled aluminum use 95 percent less energy to make, enough to run a TV for 3 hours per can!

LASTING EFFECT

Less than 2 percent of waste is recycled every year, even though half is recyclable. Getting the people in your life and community to recycle will truly help the planet!

GLOSSARY

access: a way of being able to use or get something

activist: one who acts strongly in support of or against an issue

cancer: a disease caused by the uncontrolled growth of cells in the body

environment: the conditions that surround a living thing and affect the way it lives

garbage: things that are no longer useful or wanted and have been thrown out

hazardous: involving risk or danger

infection: the spread of germs inside the body, causing illness

laser: a tool that makes a narrow beam of light

monitor: watch carefully

municipal: having to do with a city or town

sewer: a system of underground pipes that carries waste

technology: the way that people do something using tools and the tools that they use

trillion: one thousand billion

FOR MORE INFORMATION

BOOKS

Close, Edward. *What Do We Do with Trash?* New York, NY: PowerKids Press, 2013.

Dickmann, Nancy. *Leaving Our Mark: Reducing Our Carbon Footprint.* New York, NY: Crabtree Publishing, 2016.

Flynn, Sarah Wassner. *This Book Stinks! Gross Garbage, Rotten Rubbish, and the Science of Trash.* Washington, DC: National Geographic, 2017.

Tilmont, Amy. *Trash Talk: What You Throw Away.* North Mankato, MN: Norwood House Press, 2012.

Websites

Reduce, Reuse, Recycle
kids.niehs.nih.gov/topics/reduce/
Read about how you can reduce, reuse, and recycle to help protect the environment.

Waste Atlas
atlas.d-waste.com/
Search this informative world map for dumpsites.

Your Cool Facts and Tips on Waste Management
eschooltoday.com/waste-recycling/waste-management-tips-for-kids.html
Learn more about the types of waste, how they're created, and how they're managed.

31

INDEX